'S GUIDE TO

W9-DEV-241
3 4028 08459 6221
HARRIS COUNTY PUBLIC LIBRARY

MENT™

WITHDRAWN

TOP 10 SECRETS

FOR MANAGING CREDIT CARDS AND PAYING BILLS SUCCESSFULLY

THERESE SHEA

ROSEN PUBLISHING®

New York

Published in 2014 by The Rosen Publishing Group, Inc.
29 East 21st Street, New York, NY 10010

Copyright © 2014 by The Rosen Publishing Group, Inc.

First Edition

Library of Congress Cataloging-in-Publication Data

Shea, Therese.
Top 10 secrets for managing credit cards and paying bills successfully/Therese Shea.—First edition.
    pages cm.—(A student's guide to financial empowerment)
Includes bibliographical references and index.
ISBN 978-1-4488-9358-4 (library binding)—ISBN 978-1-4488-9376-8 (pbk.)—ISBN 978-1-4488-9377-5 (6-pack)
1. Credit cards—Juvenile literature. 2. Finance, Personal—Juvenile literature. 3. Consumer credit—Juvenile literature. I. Title. II. Title: Top ten secrets for managing credit cards and paying bills successfully.
HG3755.7.S54 2014
332.024'02—dc23

                                                    2013000913

Manufactured in the United States of America

CPSIA Compliance Information: Batch #S13YA: For further information, contact Rosen Publishing, New York, New York, at 1-800-237-9932.

Contents

Responsible consumers think before they use their "plastic," as people sometimes call credit cards. Credit cards can give people an artificial feeling of financial security.

Introduction

Many young people are excited when they get their first job—especially for the financial opportunities that come with a paycheck. They envision being able to buy what they need and what they want. But they should be cautious with this newfound ability. Today's culture encourages us to spend without thinking of the future. Commercials, billboards, and other advertisements persuade us to direct our money toward a variety of products and services.

Sometimes the steady income of a job means the ability to open and use a credit account. Many people are thrilled to get their first credit card. Looking at a credit limit of perhaps $1,000 or more makes the imagination run wild: Vacations! Clothes! Concert tickets! But this is how many fall into debt.

As recently as 2010, students walked into college bookstores to find tables of credit card representatives giving out T-shirts, towels, and other "gifts" to those who filled out applications. Young people needed only to open their mailboxes or e-mail accounts to find offers from credit card companies waiting. College-age students were major targets of credit card companies—and for good reason. They made credit card companies a lot of money with the debt they acquired, even if they used their cards only for books, tuition, and other necessities.

In 2009, the federal government tried to halt this slippery slope for young people. The Credit Card Accountability, Responsibility, and Disclosure (CARD) Act banned the exchange of free gifts for credit cards and urged colleges to remove credit card vendors from campuses. Under this law, people under age twenty-one now face several obstacles to getting a credit card, though many still do obtain them.

If you are one of these young people, you do not have to fall into the credit card trap. You can make credit work for you and avoid accumulating a mountain of debt. Paying your credit card and other bills helps you build the foundation for a healthy financial future. Smart use of your money can convince lenders that you have the capability to handle the debt for the car or house of your dreams. It can also help you pay for these items outright—without assuming more debt!

Many adults still struggle with debts accrued in their younger years. Some never mastered simple—though not always easy—ways to manage their bills successfully. Learning just a few rules early in your financial life can really pay off down the road.

You Might Not Need a Credit Card

Imagine that you asked someone for money every time you used a credit card. Now imagine that a month later, that person is knocking on your door asking for the money back. That is essentially what is happening when you use a credit card. Many young people think a credit card is a must. However, credit cards are not a necessity, especially for those still living at home. Before even considering a credit card, young people should ask themselves why they want one. Is it so they can have ready access to money? This is dangerous reasoning. So many people of all ages forget that credit is just a loan.

Is It Time for Credit?

There are some good reasons to get a credit card. Credit cards are handy to have in urgent situations. Young people attending college and living

Cars can be expensive when things go wrong. Many people use credit cards to pay for car repairs—but they need to be able to pay the credit card company soon afterward.

away from home might find themselves in an emergency. They might not have enough money to cover an unexpected cost, such as a car repair. In a situation like this, it makes sense to use a credit card rather than waiting and saving up the money to repair the car.

Another reason people get a credit card is to build a credit history. A credit history is a record of an individual's borrowing and repaying behaviors. Credit reports list credit card accounts, how long each has been used, amounts owed, and whether bills are paid on time. Other types of credit accounts are also included, such as mortgages and car loans. Most creditors, or the businesses to which people owe money, send monthly reports of transactions to a credit report agency, also called a credit bureau.

Other kinds of businesses, such as cell phone and utility companies, may or may not report to a credit bureau. However, if they turn over an unpaid debt to a collection agency, that will likely end up on the report. Companies often hire a collection agency to handle collection on a

Fascinating Financial Fact

Credit scores are sometimes called FICO scores because they are produced with computer software developed by Fair Isaac Corporation, or FICO. The three major U.S. credit bureaus are Experian, TransUnion, and Equifax. Each may have a different credit score for an individual as they may receive different information. FICO scores range from 300 to 850.

debt after several missed payments. Some debt agencies buy debts for less than the actual amount and then try to collect the full amount. A collection note on a credit report damages someone's credit history and remains a stain for a number of years.

Information on a credit report contributes to an overall credit score. The score is a quick way for lenders and creditors, such as credit card companies, banks, and mortgage companies, to find out if someone is likely to pay back a loan. Someone with no credit history may be considered as much of a risk as someone with a low credit score. Beginning this history is a legitimate reason to get a credit card. However, credit can be built in other ways, too, such as paying a car loan on time.

Ways to Get Credit

For those who decide they need and want a credit card, there are three ways to get one if they are under the age of twenty-one. Parents can give their children a card attached to their own accounts. This is sometimes called piggybacking. Parents are ultimately responsible for all debt incurred. If the parents have good credit habits, then children on the account will also be seen to have good credit habits. However, the opposite is true, too. Children will not benefit if parents miss payments or owe too much.

People under twenty-one can get a personal credit card account if their parents or guardians cosign for them. Cosigning also means the parent is responsible for the debt if the child does not pay the bills. Cardholders must be sure to be responsible or they risk ruining their parents' credit.

Families should help determine how credit cards figure into a young person's financial life.

It is possible for someone under twenty-one to be approved for a credit card without an adult's help. However, the CARD Act of 2009 has made it much more difficult. Because of this federal law, when a young person applies for a credit card, the card issuer must verify that he or she has significant income. Since most young people have low-paying jobs, they will not qualify for a card. Should a credit card company issue a card, the credit line—or the total amount of money the company is willing to lend the cardholder—is likely to be low.

A secured credit card is yet another way for people under twenty-one to get a card by themselves. Secured credit cards require the cardholder to place an amount of money in an account. This money acts as security for the credit issuer. If the cardholder does not pay his or her bills, the issuer can use this money. There are different rules for different secured credit cards, such as the amount of money needed in the account and the amount of credit issued. Some cards also have application fees.

A drawback is that secured credit cards often have higher interest rates than traditional cards. However, these cards are a good way for many people with damaged credit to improve their credit score. Responsible users of secured cards may find the issuer increasing their line of credit without having to place more money in the account. Some cards even become unsecured cards after a time.

Before making the jump to any credit card, it is good to establish a checking account with a debit card. It will help future credit card users become familiar with the idea of using a card with a fixed amount of money. The account will also come in handy when other kinds of bills pop up.

Read the Fine Print

If you are still interested in a credit card, you should know there are many cards out there. No one should sign up for a credit card without doing a good amount of research. Offers in the mail and online often show the enticing features of a credit card in big, colorful text (e.g. NO INTEREST FOR ONE FULL YEAR!). However attractive the large print is, people should read the small text to know exactly what they are agreeing to when they become cardholders.

Many Cards, Many Choices

Visa, MasterCard, Capital One, American Express, and Discover are some of the major credit card companies. Many banks and credit unions issue credit cards. In fact, since credit unions are not-for-profit agencies, they often charge lower interest rates and fewer fees than bank cards. Some credit card companies and banks have cards specially tailored for students. A few even offer online education programs

The process of choosing a credit card should not be taken lightly. Every credit card user is unique and should choose a card based on his or her needs and lifestyle.

for young cardholders to learn about their new financial responsibilities.

Because of the overwhelming abundance of available credit cards, some handy Web sites have been designed for easy comparison. Sites such as Bankrate.com, Credit.com, and NerdWallet.com allow people to compare details of many credit cards at once or search for cards with certain features. After someone finds a card that looks interesting, he or she should go to the card's Web site to read the most up-to-date information.

The Key Words of Credit

What details are most important in a credit card? Here are a few credit card buzzwords everyone should know.

- **APR.** This stands for annual percentage rate. It is the interest rate charged on an unpaid credit card balance over a year. Remember, the money loaned by the credit card company needs to be paid back. APR is one way a credit issuer makes money. If the cardholder does not pay off the bill fully each month, the issuer charges interest on the unpaid amount. An APR can be as high as 30 percent, but many cards offer introductory interest rates as low as 0 percent. Consumers should be sure to find out when the higher rate will kick in and what it will be. APRs can be variable or fixed. Variable rates fluctuate from month to month. Fixed rates can change but do so less frequently, and the credit card company must inform the cardholder of any changes.

- **Grace period.** A grace period is the time a cardholder is given to pay a balance before the interest, also called a finance charge, is added to it. It usually starts at the close of the monthly billing cycle and ends on the date the payment is due—usually about twenty to twenty-five days. If cardholders use their cards wisely, they can use the grace period to borrow from their issuer with no added interest.

- **Annual fee.** Some cards have an annual fee. Once a year, a charge is added to the balance on the account. Even if the cardholder does not use the card, the annual fee is applied. Why would someone want a card with an annual fee? Some cards offer rewards that exceed the cost of the annual fee. However, most people should avoid cards with this extra cost.

Fascinating Financial Fact

The use of credit cards began in the United States during the 1920s. Companies began giving them to customers to use for purchases made at their stores. Diners Club introduced the first credit card that could be used at many businesses in 1950. Some customers received a bill just once a year.

- **Late fee.** Each month, a cardholder is notified of the amount due to the credit card company, including when and how much to pay. If a user is late with a payment, he or she will find a late fee added to the balance, even if the amount owed was only a few dollars. Late fees can vary, but thanks to the CARD Act, they cannot exceed $25 per month.

- **Over-the-limit fee.** This is the fee for exceeding the credit limit of an account. For example, a card may have a credit limit of $1,000. Before the CARD Act of 2009, a credit card company could penalize a user for borrowing more than this amount. Now, a company can apply a fee only if cardholders "opt in" to be able to exceed their credit card limit. They might do this so their card is never declined. However, they should be aware of the extra fee, often $39, for going over the limit.

All of these bits of information can be found online or in the disclosure, sometimes called the terms and conditions, of a credit card information pamphlet.

Secret #3

Due Dates Matter

Even one day late is too late when it comes to credit card payments. Different cards have different policies. It is even possible to be an hour too late if a company designates a certain hour as the cutoff time! Some cards, such as American Express, provide recommended due dates, which are more than a week before the real due date in case a payment gets delayed in the mail. Cardholders should be familiar with their cards' policies.

The Drawbacks of Delay

Getting the payment to the credit card issuer on time is very important for several reasons. Credit card companies add finance charges and late fees if payments do not arrive on time. This is a way for them to profit from the money they loaned. Cardholders have the power to avoid penalties, though. Paying on time means no late fees. Paying off the full balance due each month within the grace period means no finance charges.

Fascinating Financial Fact

Before the CARD Act of 2009, a credit card issuer could increase a cardholder's interest rate if he or she was just one day late with the payment. Now the payment needs to be at least sixty days late to raise the rate on the unpaid debt. However, the company may raise the interest rate on new balances.

Late payments also affect cardholders' credit scores. Credit card companies report late payments to the credit bureaus when the payments are more than sixty days late. Unsurprisingly, such reports make a person's credit score go down. The cardholder's behavior suggests that he or she does not pay off debts responsibly. However, paying on time has a positive effect on a person's score. According to Todd Ossenfort of CreditCards.com, on-time payments account for 35 percent of a FICO credit score.

Ways to Pay

Several methods are available to pay a credit card bill. Some people send a check or money order through the mail. However, they must account for the amount of time it takes the payment to reach the company. Others pay their bills online by connecting a bank account to the credit card account. It may take a day or two for the transaction to be processed. Paying by phone is also an option. This service is free for most major credit cards. However, talking to a representative

Digital devices, such as smartphones and tablets, have made paying bills easier than ever. However you pay, you should get in the habit of taking care of your bills the same way each month.

rather than using the automated system sometimes results in an extra fee.

Getting a payment in on time may seem like a no-brainer, but many people have difficulty doing so. Life can be complicated; unplanned events occur. No matter the method they choose, cardholders should make paying off their cards as simple and easy to remember as possible. They can use smartphones and digital tablets to set reminders for themselves to pay their bills. Bank and credit card Web sites may also offer to send reminders. With online bill paying, automatic withdrawals can be set up for a certain date each month, eliminating the need for reminders.

Save the Date

The same attention given to credit card bills should be given to other bills, too. Car loans, auto insurance, rent, cell phone bills, and student loans all require on-time payments. Failure to meet the due date means a penalty of some kind, sometimes a fee or a hike in interest rates. And a very late payment, or no payment at all, may be reported to the credit bureaus. It's important to designate one or two days a month to take care of these financial responsibilities. A schedule or perhaps a digital calendar can help make paying these bills a natural part of life.

It is helpful to call companies and ask for due dates to be moved to a convenient time. For example, if you receive a paycheck on the first day of every month, it would be a smart move to request bill due dates about a week after that date. You will have money in the bank and plenty of time to get the payment in on time. With a due date several weeks later, you might spend the money and might not have enough left to pay the bills.

MYTHS
AND
FACTS

FACT

Myth
People who pay their bills on time do not need to check their credit reports.

Credit reports can contain errors. Deborah McNaughton of Professional Credit Counselors told Bankrate.com that 80 percent of all credit reports have incorrect information.

FACT

Myth
Checking a credit report will lower the score.

When a consumer checks his or her own credit report—known as a soft inquiry—it does not have an effect on the credit score. However, if a credit lender reviews the consumer's report, the score may be impacted. This is called a hard inquiry. People should check their credit reports at least annually, and they should know their score before applying for new credit.

FACT

Myth
You should always pay off credit cards and other bills before building savings.

Because carrying debt costs so much in interest and fees, many financial experts say people should always pay off debt before starting to save. However, others favor a more balanced approach. Such experts believe that without any savings, a person may fall further into debt in an emergency situation. They recommend paying off debt and building some savings at the same time.

Paying the Minimum Is a Major Mistake

Every credit card bill includes a minimum payment. While paying the minimum may seem to be the easiest route, it is the hardest in the long run. Credit card companies actually want you to pay the minimum so they can add finance charges to the unpaid balance each month. Many American consumers drown in debt from just paying the minimum. In 2003, the U.S. Office of the Comptroller asked credit card issuers to increase their minimum payments so that cardholders could pay off debts more quickly. This is still not quick enough for many.

Do the Math

How a credit card's minimum is calculated is not a secret. It is listed in the terms and conditions of the card. Usually, the minimum payment is determined in one of two ways. It may be calculated as a percentage of the total amount owed, usually between 1 and 4 percent. For example, a minimum payment might be 2 percent of a $500 balance, or $10. This sounds like a painless way to slowly pay off a credit card, right? Many people think so, but they are forgetting about the card's interest rate. Each month interest is added to the amount owed on the card. By making only minimum payments on a card with an 18 percent APR, it would take ninety-four payments, or more than seven years, to pay off a $500 balance—and about $430 in accumulated finance charges!

Payment Due Date		12/20/12
Minimum Payment Due		$25.00

Late Payment Warning: If we do not receive your minimum payment by the date listed above, you may have to pay a late fee of up to $35.00 and your APR's will be subject to increase to a maximum Penalty APR of 29.99%.

Minimum Payment Warning: If you make only the minimum payment each period, you will pay more in interest and it will take you longer to pay off your balance. For example:

If you make no additional charges using this card and each month you pay...	You will pay off the balance shown on this statement in about...	And you will end up paying an estimated total of...
Only the minimum payment	7 years	$2,072
$48	3 years	$1,731 (Savings=$341)

This credit card company warns the cardholder what will happen if he or she pays only the minimum. Remember, the faster the balance is paid off, the less interest is owed.

In other cases, the minimum payment is calculated by taking a percentage of the balance plus a monthly interest charge, which is based on the card's APR. Using the previous example of a $500 balance, the percentage of the balance will likely be low, maybe 1 percent. If the APR is 18 percent, the monthly interest rate is 1/12 of that, or 1.5 percent. That means another $7.50 is added to 1 percent of $500, or $5. The minimum payment is $12.50. A credit card may also have a fixed dollar amount, such as $15, for the minimum payment. The higher amount is the one that the cardholder is required to pay.

While these calculations are important, the crucial information for credit card users is that interest and finance charges are going to the credit card companies' profits and not to pay off their accounts. In the example above, $7.50 is the charge that the user paid to borrow $500. This is another reason to pay off all, or as much as possible, of the balance each month. A finance charge on zero is zero!

Minimum payments are also features of many other bills, such as payments for car and student loans. Such loans involve an individual borrowing a lump sum and paying it back with interest to the lender. These bills, too, have a minimum

Fascinating Financial Fact

Employers are allowed to see a version of employees' and potential employees' credit reports. Therefore, a poor credit score could be an obstacle to getting a job.

payment. To pay loans off faster, borrowers should think of the minimum as a suggestion and pay as much as they can. Sometimes paying just a bit more a month can mean shaving years off of the repayment period and hundreds, or even thousands, of dollars in savings.

New Accounts, New Concerns

Many people are lured into signing up for new credit cards because of 0 percent or low introductory APRs. Without the monthly interest charges, they are also lulled into complacency about paying off the bill in full. Users can run into trouble when the introductory period is over, though. They might be stuck with a large balance on their card and finance charges adding up every month.

Some might think it would be a good idea to close a credit card account once an introductory offer is complete or the interest rate on the card goes up. However, opening and closing cards can hurt a credit score, especially if money is owed on the account. When customers close an account, their overall line of credit goes down. As a result, the percentage of their credit line that is debt increases. Let's say you owe $500 on one account with a credit limit of $1,000 and have another card with a $1,000 credit limit. The "utilization" of your credit cards is $500 out of $2,000, or 25 percent. If you close one account, you owe $500 out of $1,000 of credit, and the utilization is 50 percent. The higher the utilization rate, the riskier a person looks to the credit bureaus and future lenders. The less available credit a person uses, the higher his or her credit score. For this reason, Bankrate.com suggests keeping balances on all credit cards under 30 percent of the credit limit. For example, for a $500 credit limit, keep balances under $150.

Some people sign up for a new credit card to transfer a balance from another card. Perhaps the new card has a lower interest rate. Users need to be careful about doing this as well. Again, read the fine print. Often, balance transfers have no grace period. That means cardholders start paying interest on that transferred balance the same day they put it on the new card. Be sure

Many businesses entice consumers to sign up for a credit card as they are checking out. They may promise additional savings, too. Consumers should not make hurried decisions about credit cards, though.

to watch for transfer fees as well, often 3 to 4 percent of the balance. Also, after getting an additional card, the sudden increase in available credit can tempt one to spend. Cardholders need to be careful not to rack up additional debt, as this will wipe out any savings from the balance transfer.

Read Statements and Bills

Not only should you look at how much you owe on a bill, you should read the entire statement to find out why you owe it. While the reading is not as interesting as the latest best seller, you may save yourself some money. It would be nice if you could trust credit card companies and other businesses to always get it right, but computers and people can make errors. And sometimes a bill can indicate a bigger problem.

Looking for Trouble

Financial advisers recommend keeping receipts until they can be checked against a credit card statement. If the receipt does not match the amount on the statement, call the place of purchase and ask the store to alter the amount. If the merchant does not deal with the situation, call the credit card company and ask what steps it can take to help you.

Fascinating Financial Fact

Though 850 is the best possible credit score, only 13 percent of the U.S. population has a FICO score greater than 800, according to myFICO.com.

Credit card users should also check their monthly statements for unfamiliar charges. These amounts might mean that someone is using the account. Thieves do not always need to steal the card. Hackers have broken into bank and other Web sites to steal numbers. There are even Web sites that sell people's card numbers. People who handle credit cards in stores and restaurants may also secretly copy card numbers.

If a card is stolen or an account is used without permission, it will not necessarily have a huge amount of money charged to it. Many thieves use cards for a long time by charging just a few dollars at a time. They are counting on people not to pay attention to their bills or to think that a few dollars are not a big deal. However, credit scores can be ruined, and much money can be lost. People should contact their credit card company immediately if they do not recognize a charge or if the amount is incorrect.

Regularly checking the credit card statement online is an even better idea than waiting for a paper copy each month. Besides looking for suspicious charges, cardholders can decide to stop using their cards when the balances become too high for that month. In addition, many companies allow

Reading credit card statements each month and checking them against receipts can save consumers money. This habit is also a good way of monitoring overall monthly expenses.

cardholders to set alerts for certain transactions or limits. For example, users can get a text or e-mail if they hit a spending limit of $200. Take advantage of these alerts to keep your balances manageable.

Be Alert

It is just as important to read other bills, such as those for phone and car payments. Mistakes can be made on these documents as well. According to CNN.com, the Federal Communications Commission (FCC) estimates that fifteen to twenty million U.S. households have received "mystery fees" on their monthly landline phone bills. In many cases, phone companies padded bills with charges for services the customers never ordered or used. They were able to do this without most customers noticing. Only 5 percent of consumers who were affected were aware of the monthly charges. Mystery charges happen on cell phone bills, too. Customers should call the phone company if they notice a problem with a bill. And if the bill seems high, they can talk to service representatives about why and adjust payment plans if necessary.

By investigating a bill, utility customers may find out that they have a faulty electric, gas, or water meter. The sooner they find the problem, the fewer money-related headaches they will have in the future.

Keep That Bill— At Least for a While

You should keep bills and receipts, and not only for checking them against your credit card statement each month. People who are financially secure are great record keepers. By keeping records of the money they have spent, they know better how to plan for the future. You can start this good habit now. Your bills and receipts can help you figure out a realistic budget. Following this budget will ensure that you have enough money to pay your bills—and some left over for fun.

Your Life, Your Budget

To calculate your budget, carry a small notebook with you for a month. Write down each of your expenses. Hang on to all bills and receipts as well. Write down the amount of each of these in your notebook. At the end of the month, find the total sum. Next, write down how much money you earn in one month. Is it less or more than your total expenses? If the amount you earned is less than the amount you spent, you have work to do on your budget and are in danger of falling into debt.

Take another look at the expenses. Create categories, such as cell phone costs, entertainment, food, clothes, and loan payments. Sort your expenditures (the various amounts you spent on different items) into these categories. Find your total spending in each category.

Decide which categories can be adjusted the next month to help you live within your income. Reducing your spending in various categories can help you save for a major purchase, pay off credit cards, or create a nest egg. Your spending in some categories cannot be adjusted much. For example, a loan payment is a set amount. However, entertainment or food categories can usually be altered. You could eat at home or go to the movies less often. You can also choose to spend a bit less in one category so you can spend a little more in another.

The next month, try sticking to your budget. You can adjust the budget as you take on new expenses, change jobs, or set a new financial goal.

Fascinating Financial Fact

Some credit cards offer a benefit known as purchase protection. The card company will reimburse customers for the cost of goods that are stolen or accidentally damaged soon after purchase (such as in the first ninety days). This is another good reason to keep receipts.

Documents to Save

Even after a budget is set, hang on to receipts, bills, and statements for a time. As previously mentioned, sales receipts should be checked against credit card statements. People should also keep receipts in case they need to return an item or take back an item that is defective. Loan statements confirm that payments are being received. Utility and phone bills help customers track and modify their use and decide whether they should switch providers.

Of course, these documents need to go somewhere for easy access. Make space in a drawer, cabinet, or closet to store bills and records. Use folders or envelopes to separate documents. Designate one day a month as the day to balance the checkbook and check your monthly receipts. It might be the same day you take care of your monthly bills. A set schedule will keep you paying your bills faithfully and make you feel more in charge of your financial life.

You do not have to hang on to receipts and statements forever. Here is a list of some financial documents people should keep and the recommended time periods for saving them:

- **Sales receipts.** Keep these until the purchase warranty for the item expires or the purchase can no longer be returned or exchanged.
- **ATM receipts.** Keep for one month; throw out after you balance your checkbook.
- **Paycheck stubs.** Keep for one year; throw out after they are checked against your tax documents.
- **Utility bills.** Keep for one year.
- **Credit card receipts.** Keep for one year.

A little time and information gathering is needed to set up a budget at first. As you become more familiar with your budget, it becomes easier to stick to the plan each month.

- **Bank statements.** Keep for one year.
- **Cancelled insurance policies and medical bills.** Keep for three years.
- **Records of paid car or student loans.** Keep for seven years.

A little organization goes a long way on the road to financial success. Many of the skills one learns in budgeting and record keeping are also necessities in the business world.

Cash Advances Are Too Good to Be True

Some people who run out of money before they get their next paycheck may think that cash advances are the answer. Many credit cards offer cash advances. A cardholder can either use the credit card at an ATM to withdraw money (which is borrowed from the credit card company) or cash a convenience check. Both charges are connected to the user's credit card account. Does that sound too good to be true? It is for most people.

A Slippery Slope into Debt

Unlike regular credit purchases, cash advances have no grace period. This means the borrowed amount begins accruing interest the same day the money is withdrawn or the check is cashed. Typically, a cash advance has a higher interest rate than the card's regular line of credit. On top of that, there is often a fee for the transaction. All these conditions of cash advances are listed on a credit card's monthly statement and on convenience checks, but consumers often overlook the fine print.

These three features of the cash advance—the lack of a grace period, the higher interest rate, and the user fee—means debt increases swiftly. According to Credit.com, an average consumer receiving a $2,000 cash advance can expect to pay about $100 in fees and about $40 in interest in just one month. Generally, cash advances should be a last resort. Ask family and friends for a loan before getting a cash advance. And if you really must get one, pay it off as quickly as possible.

You can think of cash advances as very short-term loans. They are offered by most credit card companies and can be accessed through ATMs. The interest rate and fees are often high.

Emergency Funds: One Step Ahead

There will always be unexpected costs in life: car repairs, trips to the hospital, and other unforeseen needs. Sometimes they pop up at the worst times. Preparing for the future is one

Fascinating Financial Fact

In 2012, the number of Americans who reported having no emergency fund rose to 28 percent, according to Bankrate.com's Financial Security Index survey.

of the smartest things someone can do. Instead of putting yourself in the position of needing a cash advance, it is wise to build an emergency fund.

There are several ways you can build an emergency fund. If you get a steady paycheck, remove an amount each month and add it to the fund. You might not even have to do it yourself: you can set up an automatic payment to move money from your checking account to a savings account. Another method is to find a monthly expense that can be easily cut from your budget. For example, if you treat yourself to cocoa every morning at the local coffee shop, try making it at home instead. Put that money toward the fund each morning instead. Even placing the change in your pocket into a jar each day can add up over time.

How much money should be in an emergency fund? Experts suggest that adults have at least six months of expenses covered. Take a look at your budget to figure out your expenses for one month. Now multiply it by six. That might seem like a lot, but it means you will not have to panic if you lose your job or if an emergency comes your way. An emergency fund can be the difference between financial security and a lifetime of debt.

Pick Up the Phone

You might be surprised to hear that your credit card company needs you. Remember, companies earn money from customers: no customers, no profits. Therefore you have a certain amount of power in your relationship with your credit card company. How can you use this power? For one thing, you might be able to lower your interest rate.

Reducing Rates and Fighting Fees

Unless a card has a variable rate, interest rates are locked in for a period of time after opening a credit account. This is typically one year, or less for cards with a promotional rate. After that, the issuer needs only to inform the cardholder that the rate is going up. There is no maximum interest rate according to federal law.

Card companies take advantage of delinquency, raising rates as a penalty without a formal warning if the cardholder has not paid in sixty days. However, the CARD Act helps the cardholder who gets back

Speaking to a customer service representative is often the fastest way to resolve a problem or get an answer to a question about a bill.

on track. If the cardholder makes the next six payments on time following the rate hike, the company must reduce the rate again, though it does not need to go back to the original rate. Once more, it pays to be timely with bills.

Cardholders can call their credit company and speak to a representative about lowering the interest rate. They should mention any offers from another credit card company with a lower interest rate. They should keep the conversation pleasant and respectful at all times and ask to talk to a supervisor if needed. Credit card companies want to keep good customers, so it can't hurt to ask.

Cardholders can also ask the company to waive a fee. For example, if they are late for a payment and it is an unusual occurrence for them, they should call a customer service representative and explain why. In some circumstances, companies may forgive a late fee. Some people have also had luck getting a reduction in a credit card's annual fee. A history of good credit is always helpful in these situations.

Ask for Aid Before It's Too Late

So what can people do if they are not perfect customers? What can they do if they have acquired a large credit card debt and are feeling panicked about how to pay it off? Again, call the company and speak to a representative. Many companies have debt repayment plans. They may ask for information about the customer's monthly budget. Then they may freeze or lower the customer's interest rate. The company will not reduce the amount owed. However, it can help determine how much the customer needs to pay each month in order to settle the debt in a specified amount of time. Cardholders should call before they miss a payment, as this may affect the interest rate as well as add late fees. The drawback to a repayment plan is that it usually involves

This drawer of cut-up credit cards is located in a credit counseling agency. Sometimes the first step in getting out of debt is ending the line of credit.

Fascinating Financial Fact

According to CreditCards.com, of the U.S. households that had credit card debt in 2012, the average amount owed was $15,799.

closing the account. Also, credit scores may take a hit. But these consequences are better than a snowballing debt.

In fact, it pays to pick up the phone no matter what bill faces you. Always take action before the payment is due to avoid added fees. A customer representative may be able to extend the due date or waive a late fee. Be sure to note the representative's name and the date and time of the conversation in case it is needed later. Remember, all bills are important to pay, but creditors and lenders that report to credit bureaus—including providers of mortgages, student loans, credit cards, and car loans—can affect your credit score for years to come. Overdue payments can end up on your credit report if a loan goes into default or unpaid bills are passed to a collection agency.

When people find themselves in crushing debt, going to a credit counseling agency is a possibility. For a fee, these organizations offer debt counseling, repayment plans, and budgeting advice. The Federal Trade Commission (FTC) publishes a series of free publications on credit and financial issues and is a good resource for finding a reputable credit counselor.

1   I lost my job. How do I pay my bills?

2   I've been late paying my credit card bill a few times. Should I be worried about my credit score?

3   What is the biggest mistake that most people make with their credit cards?

4   If I don't have enough money to cover all of my bills, which have the fewest repercussions for lateness?

5   I think someone has been using my credit cards. What steps should I take if I think I'm the victim of identity theft?

6   How does a debt repayment plan work, and are there fees involved?

7   How do I find more money in my budget to pay off bills?

8   I was the victim of identity theft. What can I do to make sure it doesn't happen again?

9   I have two different credit card bills. Should I first pay off the bigger debt with the lower interest rate or the smaller debt with the higher interest rate?

10   How do I stop myself from spending too much money on entertainment and nonessential items?

Be Careful with Personal Information

Someday, someone may open a credit card account with your name. They may use your Social Security number. They may use some other piece of personal information for their financial gain. You may get a bill in the mail for a card you do not have. If so, you are the victim of a crime called identity theft.

Take Action

If you think you may be the victim of identity theft, the first thing you need to do is contact one of the three major credit bureaus to place a fraud alert on your account. These organizations and their phone numbers are:

- TransUnion: (800) 680-7289
- Equifax: (800) 525-6285
- Experian: (888) EXPERIAN [397-3742]

Each agency will contact the others. You will also have to contact and close the accounts that have been used. The police should be informed as well. They will guide you in the steps to take to clear your name and credit history.

Keep It Classified

Even someone who has excellent credit, a healthy budget, and a large savings can get into financial trouble by being careless with personal information. According to a survey by Javelin Strategy & Research, more than

A shredder is a useful tool to keep information from getting into the wrong hands. Some shredders are strong enough to slice credit cards.

11.6 million people became victims of identity fraud in the United States in 2011, an increase of 13 percent over the prior year. The company's report blames social media and mobile technology for the rise. Increasingly, hackers can break into secure Web sites that hold information such as Social Security numbers and debit and credit card numbers.

Though you cannot do much about hacking, you can protect yourself from identity theft in other ways. First, do not give anyone usernames or passwords. Do not save this data on your computer, in case someone steals the computer or breaks through the firewall. Spyware is made just for this sinister purpose. Be sure to install some kind of antivirus/anti-spyware program. Take steps to secure all smartphones and digital devices as well. Most people do not use a password on the home screen of their phones, but this action can be helpful.

Do not disclose too much information about yourself on social networking sites. Others can use facts such as birthdays, addresses, and even pets' names to "prove" they are you. Be suspicious of e-mails and phone calls that claim to be from banks and ask for information such as pin numbers. This is a common technique to gather information illegally.

When throwing away documents, put them through a shredder if possible. At the very least, destroy any parts of a document that contain a Social Security number or other personal information.

Fascinating Financial Fact

According to Javelin Strategy & Research, 43 percent of fraud cases in 2011 were first discovered by the victims. This indicates the importance of checking accounts often and not trusting that someone else will detect the identity theft.

Be on the Lookout

Finally, check all bank and credit accounts frequently to make sure no one else is using them. People can and should get a free copy of their credit report once a year at http://www.annualcreditreport.com. You can check the information in your report to see if anything seems odd. If something does look suspicious, act immediately. Credit reporting agencies are required by law to fix errors, and an error may indicate identity theft.

What if your credit card is lost or stolen? Call the credit card company immediately. Luckily, under the Fair Credit Billing Act, cardholders are liable for only $50 in charges if a thief uses their card right away, and no money at all after the card is reported lost. For this reason, keep a record of all account numbers, expiration dates, and the telephone number of each card issuer so you can report a loss quickly. After the incident, review billing statements carefully. If they show any unauthorized purchases, send a letter to the card issuer describing each questionable charge and requesting a refund. Keep a copy of the correspondence.

The loss of a debit card can be even more serious. A thief could steal all the money in your bank account. If it is possible that the card is only misplaced, the company can freeze the account temporarily if you wish. Always act as quickly as possible. Check out the FTC's Web site for more information about the federal laws that offer protection. In addition, many credit cards offer their own consumer protection programs; these can be found in their terms and conditions.

Always Think Ahead

It can be hard to resist the impulse to buy, but always think ahead. Marketers make goods and services seem so appealing. However, avoiding the urge to buy unnecessary things is another way to avoid credit card and other kinds of debt. Whether you are the kind of consumer to buy one expensive item or many inexpensive items, you should know both can be dangerous.

Big and Small, Good and Bad Debt

A big-ticket item such as a flat-screen television can take months or years to pay off, depending on your budget. Remember, if the entire amount is not paid when the bill comes, the remaining sum collects interest. Expensive items do not have to be off-limits, but a financial plan should be in place before they are purchased. Saving up and buying with cash is the best plan, perhaps when the item is on sale. But if that is not possible, another kind of plan should be implemented to pay off the credit card quickly.

Sales are an effective way for businesses to tempt consumers to buy goods on impulse that they may not have purchased otherwise.

Small-ticket items can be a problem, too. Some people use their credit cards to buy a snack or lunch each day. After a month, this can add up on a credit card. It may have been enough to pay another bill. And if the cardholder can't pay off the full amount owed on the card, these small items may cost much more in the long run. A less obvious, but perhaps bigger, problem indicated by frequent small impulse purchases is an overall attitude of thinking, "It's just a few bucks." Most people who use credit to buy small-ticket items do so often. It becomes a habit, and like any bad habit, it has negative consequences.

Financial experts separate debt into two categories: good and bad. Good debt funds things that are valuable for the future, for example, student loans and home mortgages. An education will probably lead to a higher paying job. A home can increase in value and provide the security of a place to live for years to come. Bad debt is accumulated through disposable purchases. Goods like a cup of coffee do not change the buyer's life much, and the buyer has nothing to show for it after it is consumed. These categories may be helpful to consider as you control your impulse to buy. In addition, ask these questions: Is the purchase going to improve my life? Is the purchase supposed to make me feel better? Is there another way to fill this need? Is there something else I want to use this money for?

Another way to avoid an impulse purchase is to allow time to think about it. Sometimes just walking away for a few hours or a night of sleep can make people rethink priorities. Other people simply leave their credit cards at home. If they do not have the cash, they cannot make an impulse purchase with credit. Some people even freeze their credit cards in ice. If they want to use them, they have to wait for them to thaw!

More Fine Print

Many stores urge people to give in to their desires for big-ticket items by promising them they will not have to pay until later. Stores bank on the possibility that people will not have the money later. When the interest-free period is over, they often charge outrageous interest rates as well as transaction fees. Consumers should read the fine print of any credit contract to educate themselves.

Many retail stores also push their own credit cards, offering the customer a discount on the initial purchase. This is yet

Fascinating Financial Fact

Millennials, or those people born between 1980 and 1995, are 52 percent more likely than people in other generations to report making unplanned purchases simply to spoil themselves, according to a 2012 survey by the Integer Group, a brand research firm.

another way to encourage the impulse buyer. Unfortunately, store credit cards typically have higher interest rates than the major credit cards.

Another drawback is a hit to the user's credit score. Opening a new credit account lowers the overall score. The older the average age of an individual's credit accounts, the better his or her score will be. People who are thinking about getting a loan for a car or home in the next year should think twice about opening a new card. People with good credit scores might get bumped down several points. Getting several new cards in a short period of time can cause an even bigger drop. Is that 15 percent off at the clothes shop or electronics store worth it? In an interview with Bankrate.com, Andy Jolls, a former executive at FICO, put it into perspective: "Be careful to not trade $50 in savings now for $50 more in a mortgage payment per month for the next thirty years."

Face the Future

Weighing your money choices now with the consequences you may face in the future is the single most important tip you can keep in mind. It may sound simple, but it can help

A good credit score can help car buyers obtain a loan with a low interest rate. Healthy financial habits have positive consequences throughout a person's life.

you make the right decisions. Practicing good money habits now will allow you to have more money in your pocket at the end of the month, as well as better credit in the future. Smart credit card users who pay off their balances quickly are rewarded with good credit scores and low-interest loans for big-ticket items, such as houses and cars. With similar habits, they can pay off these items quickly, too. This means more wealth for them and less money paid in interest to lenders. Wise use of a credit card can teach you good habits for a successful financial life.

Glossary

accrue To increase in amount.

automated Running or operating using machines or electronics rather than human labor.

balance The amount of money available in a financial account, such as a bank account; also, the amount of money owed on a financial account, such as a credit card.

complacency The condition of being satisfied without being aware of possible dangers.

credit score A number that lenders use to determine the credit risk you pose and the interest rate they will offer you if they agree to lend you money.

credit union A cooperative savings association that makes loans to its members at reduced interest rates.

default Failure to meet a financial or legal obligation, especially to repay a loan.

delinquency Failure to make a payment on a debt or obligation by the specified due date.

disclosure The act of making information known.

firewall Hardware or software designed to prevent unauthorized access to a computer system.

fraud The crime of obtaining something by deception.

hacker A person who uses computer skills to gain unauthorized access to a computer system belonging to another.

incur To bring something upon oneself as a result of one's actions.

interest rate The amount charged by a lender to a borrower for the use of money.

liable Having legal responsibility for costs and damages.

penalize To punish someone for breaking a rule.

repercussion A problem that results from an action.

spyware Software that is installed on a computer without the user's knowledge to gather information about an individual or organization.

vendor Someone who sells something.

waive To give up voluntarily.

For More Information

Bankrate, Inc.
11760 U.S. Highway 1, Suite 200
North Palm Beach, FL 33408
(561) 630-2400
Web site: http://www.bankrate.com
Bankrate, Inc., is one of the most trusted publishers of
    financial news.

The Brockman Institute
P.O. Box 9888
Fountain Valley, CA 92728
(949) 559-1915
Web site: http://www.brockmaninstitute.com
This organization focuses on helping at-risk and low-income
    young adults. It empowers them to take control of their
    futures through financial literacy education and other
    programs.

Canadian Bankers Association (CBA)
Box 348, Commerce Court West
199 Bay Street, 30th Floor
Toronto, ON M5L 1G2
Canada
(416) 362-6092
Web site: http://www.yourmoney.cba.ca

The Your Money program of the Canadian Bankers
Association is a financial program and resource especially tailored for young Canadians. The Web site has
information for youth, teachers, and parents.

Canadian Centre for Financial Literacy
60 St. Clair Avenue East, Suite 700
Toronto, ON M4T 1N5
Canada
(416) 665-2828
Web site: http://www.theccfl.ca
The Canadian Centre for Financial Literacy is dedicated to
supporting financial literacy across Canada. It aids
organizations that provide training and education to
Canada's low-income citizens.

Federal Trade Commission (FTC)
600 Pennsylvania Avenue NW
Washington, DC 20580
(202) 326-2222
Web site: http://www.ftc.gov
The FTC's Web site is the best place for finding information
about how to protect yourself from identity theft and
how to respond if it happens to you.

National Foundation for Credit Counseling (NFCC)
2000 M Street NW, Suite 505
Washington, DC 20036

(202) 677-4300

Web site: http://www.nfcc.org

The National Foundation for Credit Counseling promotes financially responsible behavior through financial education and counseling services. It is the nation's largest and longest-serving nonprofit credit counseling organization.

Web Sites

Due to the changing nature of Internet links, Rosen Publishing has developed an online list of Web sites related to the subject of this book. This site is updated regularly. Please use this link to access the list:

http://www.rosenlinks.com/SGFE/CC

For Further Reading

Arrowood, Janet C. *Financial Success for Young Adults and Recent Graduates: Managing Money, Credit, and Your Future.* Lanham, MD: Rowman & Littlefield Education, 2006.

Bajtelsmit, Vickie L., and Linda G. Rastelli. *Personal Finance* (Wiley Pathways). Hoboken, NJ: John Wiley & Sons, 2008.

Bedford/St. Martin's. *Insider's Guide to Credit Cards.* New York, NY: Bedford/St. Martin's, 2011.

Blumenthal, Karen. *The Wall Street Journal Guide to Starting Your Financial Life.* New York, NY: Three Rivers Press, 2009.

Byers, Ann. *First Credit Cards and Credit Smarts* (Get Smart with Your Money). New York, NY: Rosen Publishing, 2010.

Espejo, Roman. *Teens and Credit* (At Issue). Detroit, MI: Greenhaven Press, 2010.

Hamilton, Jill. *Money Management* (Issues That Concern You). Detroit, MI: Greenhaven Press, 2009.

Hunt, Mary. *7 Money Rules for Life: How to Take Control of Your Financial Future.* Grand Rapids, MI: Revell, 2012.

La Bella, Laura. *How Consumer Credit and Debt Work* (Real World Economics). New York, NY: Rosen Publishing, 2013.

Leonard, Robin, and Margaret Reiter. *Solve Your Money Troubles: Debt, Credit & Bankruptcy.* 13th ed. Berkeley, CA: Nolo, 2011.

Minden, Cecilia. *Using Credit Wisely* (Real World Math: Personal Finance). Ann Arbor, MI: Cherry Lake Publishing, 2008.

Riggs, Thomas, and Mary Bonk. *Everyday Finance: Economics, Personal Money Management, and Entrepreneurship.* Detroit, MI: Gale Cengage Learning, 2008.

Trejos, Nancy. *Hot (Broke) Messes: How to Have Your Latte and Drink It, Too.* New York, NY: Business Plus, 2010.

Weisman, Steve. *50 Ways to Protect Your Identity in a Digital Age: New Financial Threats You Need to Know and How to Avoid Them.* 2nd ed. Upper Saddle River, NJ: FT Press, 2013.

Weston, Liz Pulliam. *Deal with Your Debt: Free Yourself from What You Owe.* Rev. ed. Upper Saddle River, NJ: Financial Times/Prentice Hall, 2013.

Weston, Liz Pulliam. *Your Credit Score, Your Money & What's at Stake: How to Improve the 3-Digit Number That Shapes Your Financial Future.* Upper Saddle River, NJ: FT Press, 2010.

Bibliography

Bankrate.com. "11 Credit Report Myths." June 9, 2008. Retrieved August 10, 2012 (http://www.bankrate.com/finance/debt/11-credit-report-myths-1.aspx).

Burns-Millyard, Kathy. "How to Figure Out a Home Budget." TheNest.com. Retrieved August 3, 2012 (http://budgeting.thenest.com/figure-out-home-budget-3438.html).

Clark, Ken. *The Complete Idiot's Guide to Getting Out of Debt.* New York, NY: Alpha Books, 2009.

Dratch, Dana. "8 Little-Known Facts About Your Credit Card." Bankrate.com. Retrieved July 17, 2012 (http://www.bankrate.com/finance/credit-cards/little-known-facts-credit-card.aspx).

Gahran, Amy. "FCC Moves to Fight Mystery Fees on Your Phone Bill." CNN.com, June 20, 2011. Retrieved July 20, 2012 (http://www.cnn.com/2011/TECH/mobile/06/20/phone.bill.cramming.gahran/index.html).

Harzog, Beverly Blair. "Credit Card Q & A: How Do Cash Advances on Credit Cards Work?" Credit.com, January 3, 2011. Retrieved July 22, 2012 (http://www.credit.com/blog/2011/01/credit-card-qanda-how-do-cash-advances-on-credit-cards-work).

Harzog, Beverly Blair. "7 Secrets of Credit Card Companies." MSN Money, December 5, 2011. Retrieved July 22, 2012 (http://money.msn.com/credit-cards/7-secrets-of-credit-card-companies-credit.aspx).

Herron, Janna. "Twelve Tips to Manage Credit Card Debt in 2012." Fox Business, January 9, 2012. Retrieved July 30, 2012 (http://www.foxbusiness.com/personal-finance /2012/01/09/twelve-tips-to-manage-credit-card -debt-in-2012).

HowStuffWorks.com. "How Credit Cards Work." Retrieved July 25, 2012 (http://money.howstuffworks.com/personal -finance/debt-management/credit-card.htm).

Investopedia.com. "What Is the Highest Achievable FICO Score?" May 14, 2008. Retrieved July 10, 2012 (http:// www.investopedia.com/ask/answers/07/FICO-score .asp#ixzz1zltx9ZFc).

Irby, LaToya. "The Consequences of Skipped Payments." About.com. Retrieved July 19, 2012 (http://credit.about .com/od/buildingcredit/qt/creditpayment.htm).

Irby, LaToya. "How to Choose a Secured Credit Card." About .com. Retrieved July 20, 2012 (http://credit.about .com/od/usingcreditcards/bb/securedcard.htm).

Javelin Strategy & Research. "Identity Fraud Rose 13 Percent in 2011 According to New Javelin Strategy & Research Report." February 22, 2012. Retrieved July 16, 2012 (https://www.javelinstrategy.com/news/1314/92/Identity -Fraud-Rose-13-Percent-in-2011-According-to-New -Javelin-Strategy-Research-Report/d,pressRoomDetail).

McFadden, Leslie. "Does Law Cap Credit Card Interest Rates?" Bankrate.com. Retrieved July 18, 2012 (http:// www.bankrate.com/finance/credit-cards/does-law-cap -credit-card-interest-rates.aspx#ixzz20cVU1AUa).

McFadden, Leslie. "Store Credit Card: Good Deal?" Bankrate.com. Retrieved July 17, 2012 (http://www.bankrate.com/finance/credit-cards/store-credit-card-good-deal-1.aspx#ixzz20SLTptT6).

Michael, Paul. "The Dirty Secrets of Credit Cards." Wise Bread, March 7, 2007. Retrieved July 25, 2012 (http://www.wisebread.com/the-dirty-secrets-of-credit-cards).

Opdyke, Jeff D. *The Wall Street Journal Complete Personal Finance Guidebook.* New York, NY: Three Rivers Press, 2006.

Orman, Suze. "Managing Debt: Financial Clutter: What to Keep and What to Get Rid Of." SuzeOrman.com. Retrieved August 5, 2012 (http://www.suzeorman.com/igsbase/igstemplate.cfm?SRC=MD012&SRCN=aoedetails&GnavID=84&SnavID=20&TnavID=&AreasofExpertiseID=17).

Ossenfort, Todd. "Late Credit Card Payments Don't Justify Instant Rate Hikes Anymore." CreditCards.com, April 5, 2010. Retrieved August 4, 2012 (http://www.creditcards.com/credit-card-news/ossenfort-late-credit-card-payment-interest-increase-1292.php).

Sandberg, Erica. "Getting a Credit Card at Age 18 Isn't Easy." CreditCards.com, August 3, 2011. Retrieved July 16, 2012 (http://www.creditcards.com/credit-card-news/erica-sandberg-getting-credit-cards-age-18-1377.php).

Steiner, Sheyna. "Do You Have Emergency Savings?" MSN Money, June 25, 2012. Retrieved August 3, 2012 (http://money.msn.com/family-money/article.aspx?post=97699cb9-c562-4b20-9577-97a0a205212e).

Travis, Sean. "7 Credit Card Management Tips for College Students." SecuredCreditCardsOnline.com, April 30, 2012. Retrieved July 15, 2012 (http://secured creditcardsonline.com/7-credit-card-management -tips-for-college-students).

Tuttle, Brad. "Millennials Make Selfish Impulse Buys More Than Other Age Groups." TIME.com, April 27, 2012. Retrieved August 8, 2012 (http://moneyland.time.com/2012/ 04/27/millennials-are-biggest-suckers-for-selfish -impulse-buys).

USA.gov. "Credit—Out of Control Debt." Retrieved July 20, 2012 (http://www.usa.gov/topics/money/credit/debt/ out-of-control.shtml).

Weston, Liz. "Does Your Teen Need a Credit Card?" MSN Money, September 14, 2011. Retrieved August 4, 2012 (http://money.msn.com/credit-cards/does-your-teen -need-a-credit-card-weston.aspx).

Index

About the Author

Therese Shea, an author and former educator, has written over one hundred books on a wide variety of subjects, including several on the use of math and technology in real-world applications. She holds degrees from Providence College and the State University of New York at Buffalo. The author currently resides in Atlanta, Georgia, with her husband, Mark.

Photo Credits

Cover wavebreakmedia /Shutterstock.com; pp. 4–5 Steven Puetzer/Photographer's Choice/Getty Images; p. 8 iStockphoto/Thinkstock; pp. 10, 25 © AP Images; p. 13 Nick Wright/Photolibrary/Getty Images; p. 18 Wavebreak Media/Thinkstock; p. 28 Tooga/Taxi/Getty Images; p. 33 Richard Elliott/Taxi/Getty Images; p. 35 BananaStock/Thinkstock; p. 38 Big Cheese Photo/ Thinkstock; p. 39 Nhat V. Meyer/MCT/Landov; p. 43 Martin Poole/Digital Vision/Getty Images; p. 47 Bloomberg/Getty Images; p. 50 Jupiterimages/Pixland/ Thinkstock; back cover, multiple interior pages background image iStockphoto/Thinkstock.

Designer: Michael Moy; Editor: Andrea Sclarow Paskoff; Photo Researcher: Amy Feinberg